Empath's Astrology

Discover What Your Sign Says About You and Your Future

JUN 23 2018

Disclaimer:

Table of Contents

Introduction

Thank you for downloading the book, *"Empath's Astrology: Discover what your sign says about you and your future."*

This book contains useful information about the link between empaths and astrology—a topic that is not often discussed. This book will enlighten you about how your stars impact your life, how the planets' movements affect your attitude and emotions, and how practically every object in the heavens contribute to your experiences here on Earth— whether or not you're an empath. There is a big, mysterious world out there, and though you may not know it, it influences your life in many different ways. This book will tell you how and what you can do to use those influences to your advantage. Another book that has been helpful in our knowledge to discover ourselves is <u>Psychic Empath</u>, which helps to better understand what an Empath is, and how to understand yourself.

Empaths are special beings, different from most. And don't you think it's wonderful how we are all so different from each other, yet can live together in peaceful harmony, as if we were pieces of a jigsaw puzzle that make a wonderful piece when put up together? This book will help you find your place in that puzzle where you can explore yourself and reach your full potential, giving power and substance to that space you occupy.

Again, thanks for downloading this book, I hope you enjoy it!

Chapter 1
What is an Empath?

Empathy is the ability to put yourself in someone else's shoes and experience their feelings and emotions as if they were your own. Being an empath has its upsides and downsides: your empathic abilities can be beneficial in helping others and the environment, but it can also weigh you down and drain you, leaving you feeling empty and lost.

Empaths are exceptional human beings. Their halo shines bright and attracts other souls. They're the ones who really care and listen. They are well attuned to the environment and cannot bear to witness cruelty. They have an inherent ability to feel and perceive others through their strong sense of intuition. However, due to these abilities, empaths also often experience unpleasant symptoms such as chronic fatigue, unexplained body pains, and environmental sensitivities.

If you're an empath, then you are most probably familiar with the experiences mentioned above, as well as with the following:

- You absorb people's feelings like a sponge and take them as your own.
- You feel physical and mental fatigue with no clear cause.
- You cannot stand violence and damages inflicted upon other humans, animals, and the environment.
- You feel other people's physical pain in your own body.
- You tend to become easily drained and overwhelmed in crowded places.
- Your emotional state can be unstable throughout a day. You can appear moody, aloof, and disconnected.
- People with problems often come to you for aid and guidance.
- Solitude is necessary for you; it refreshes and recharges your batteries.
- You tend to feel like you bear the weight of the world.

- You are an excellent listener and a caring, nurturing person.
- You seem to attract children and animals.
- You are highly sensitive and perceptive of your physical environment, e.g., to touch, tastes, odors, sounds, etc.
- You are highly fond of animals and nature.
- It is impossible for you to do things you don't enjoy.
- You get bored or easily distracted if what you're doing is not interesting or stimulating.
- You like travel, adventure, and freedom. You are a free spirit!

Being an empath is not a trait that can be learned. You are either an empath or you're not. Knowing and understanding your nature will enable you to make the most out of your abilities.

10 Types of Empaths

There are several types of empaths, each having its unique set of gifts and abilities. It is important to be able to define and give a name to all that we experience so that we can better understand our true nature and learn how to use our gifts to help and guide others, which could perhaps be the real purpose of our existence.

1. Claircognizant Empaths

Related to clairvoyance *(clear seeing)* and clairaudience *(clear hearing)*, claircognizance denotes *clear knowing*. Claircognizant or intuitive empaths have the capacity to acquire information, at one glance, from people around them without the need for a conversation. They can tell when someone is telling the truth, being deceptive, or hiding something, as they have this special ability to sense the hidden meanings or intentions behind the words people say.

Claircognizant empaths don't always need reason or logic to understand things; they just *know*. They are able to easily comprehend the energy of other people, and they know when something needs to be done or not.

2. Physically Receptive Empaths

Physically receptive empaths, also called medical empaths, can sense and perceive other people's physical ailments and suffering. They can pick up the energy of people's bodies and take on their symptoms and illnesses, which can often lead to unexplainable health problems.

This type of empath can feel easily drained in the midst of hostile people or situations. The pain, stress, and emotions can easily manifest through their body. This ability, however, can be especially useful in healing. As they have this certain awareness in their body. Physical empaths make good healers in both conventional and alternative medical professions.

3. Emotionally Receptive Empaths

Emotionally receptive empaths are one of the most common types. Empaths of this kind can easily pick up and take on the emotions of other people around them even before they express it. They deeply feel others' emotions as if they were theirs. For instance, an emotionally receptive empath can experience unfounded sadness around another person who is deeply sad.

If you're an emotional empath, it is important that you learn to tell your own feelings and emotions apart from others'. This will allow you to use your unique ability to help other people without becoming exhausted.

4. Fauna Empaths

Fauna empaths have a deep, strong connection with our friends from the animal world. They can hear, feel, and telepathically communicate with the creature. They know what animals need and when they need it. They have the ability to perceive and understand the emotions and mental state of an animal to the extent where they can easily interact with the animal and positively influence its behavior.

These empaths usually like to spend more time with animals than with people. Their deep mutual understanding with the animal species can also be useful in becoming an animal healer. Their special gifts can enable them to identify an animal's sickness and administer proper treatment as necessary.

5. Flora Empaths

Flora (or plant) empaths have an intuitive sense as to what plants need. They have the capability to communicate with different trees and plants by receiving their signals. If you're a plant empath, you are most likely green-fingered and would know where to properly place a plant in your home or garden. Many flora empaths put their special abilities to good use by opting to work in gardens, parks, and greenhouses. Anywhere that brings them closer and keeps them around plants.

6. Geomantic Empaths

Also called environmental empaths, geomantic empaths are the readers of earth's energy. They are attuned to the physical landscape and are drawn to certain places, often to old houses, churches, sacred stones, and groves, with no apparent reason. They can sense the happiness or sorrow a certain place holds and perceive the events that happened there.

Geomantic empaths can read energy and signals transmitted from the earth and are thus able to feel or predict an impending natural disaster. They have a profound connection to the natural world. They grieve for the cut-down trees, destroyed landscapes, and other damages inflicted upon nature.

If you're a geomantic empath, you may feel the need to recharge by spending time in nature. Filling your house with natural scents and plants may bring you more ease and happiness and helping in environmental projects can be very therapeutic for you.

7. Medium Empaths

Medium empaths have established a deep connection with the spiritual world and the supernatural. They are able to see, hear, and feel the spirits of the deceased. They can perceive the thoughts and impressions of, and may be able communicate to, entities beyond the physical/natural realm. Mediums have an extra-sensory perception of the high-frequency energies some people possess.

8. Precognitive Empaths

Empaths with precognitive abilities can foretell upcoming events or situations. They have a vision about future occurrences which are usually presented to them through dreams. Their strong intuitive sense allows them to see exactly what is going to happen or receive signals relevant to future events.

9. Telepathic Empaths

Telepathy, also called *thought transference*, is the transferring of ideas and information between individuals by means other than the five known senses. Telepathic empaths thereby have the power to accurately read and decode other people's unexpressed thoughts and ideas.

10. Psychometric Empaths

Psychometric empaths are able to receive energy, information, memories, and impressions from physical, inanimate objects such as clothing, photographs, jewelry, etc.

Being an empathetic soul is a gift, more than anything. With self-awareness, you can learn to embrace and appreciate your unique gifts and put them to best use.

Chapter 2
Empaths and Astrology

Have you ever felt different from most people around you? Do you feel things that others have not the slightest idea of? Have you ever been told that you are "too sensitive" and have to "toughen up"? If you answered yes, you most likely are an empath.

As empaths, we all have unique abilities within, which may still be underlying and are just waiting to be discovered. Being an empath can be awfully difficult, but not knowing that you are one can be even more taxing. Simple activities, such as driving on a busy highway, walking around a crowded mall, and dining in a noisy restaurant, can be anywhere from distressing to terrifying to a hypersensitive individual. This hypersensitivity can interfere with day-to-day life if not handled properly.

Astrology is an incredibly complex subject and there is a full range of tendencies and prospects as revealed by the planetary placements in the charts. Mars can sit on Aries and make you resolute with strong determination, but Neptune can take its position in Libra and turn you into a softie. Your Leo ascendant can make you appear to be extroverted and enthusiastic but your 12th House in Cancer will make you want nothing but to be home in the comfort of your inner world.

Empaths, as extraordinary and complicated beings, can gain a lot from studying astrology in terms of giving meaning to what they experience and what to do about those experiences. They can learn strategies to become stronger and more resilient, and to be able to use their empathic abilities without losing their center.

The Most Empathic Signs

The water signs—Pisces, Cancer, and Scorpio—are said to be the most empathic signs because they can feel everything. They know how someone is feeling and feel the other person's physical symptoms simply by being around them. The water sign Virgo, and earth signs Capricorn and Taurus are the second most empathic. Libra—an air sign which seeks harmony and balance—is also said to be more empathic than the others.

On the contrary, Aries, Sagittarius, and Leo, with their fiery nature, tend to focus more on the *Self* and can sometimes display a lack of empathy. It is ideal that these signs find and establish a good balance between self-awareness and the awareness of other people's needs, which shall allow for a more harmonious collaboration and communication despite diversity.

But, not being a water sign does not necessarily mean that you are incapable of empathic sensitivities. It also depends on the quantity and the placement of the water signs in your birth chart. So, do not confuse yourself into thinking you must not be an empath and must not be overwhelmed with empathic abilities. You may have water overflowing from different places in your chart, inundating you with empathic tendencies you may not even be aware of!

It is extremely important for empaths to know that they are indeed empaths so that they can start learning how to properly shield their energy fields and not be drained all the time. Empathy and sensitivity are a beautiful thing as it can help you understand others and allow you to build a healthy connection with them. Just know how to set well-defined boundaries in order for you to still maintain a strong sense of your *Self*.

What types of Empath are you based on your sign?

Below is a list of the signs and the type of empath they most likely are, based on how their stars align among the other stars and the planets in the sky.

Aries: You are an intellectual empath to whom people often go to for advice. You have the ability to really go deep into what you are saying and make your points explained properly and clearly. You talk things through with people who really need your help.

Taurus: You are an emotional empath who tends to take on things more deeply than other kinds of empaths do, which can take a toll on you. It is important that you learn to get your emotions under control and set boundaries on your selflessness.

Gemini: You are an empath who just knows things. Your sense of intuition is so spot-on, and you use it as a way to help people in ways others cannot. You also know when something needs to be done for someone.

Cancer: You are an empath who loves being out in nature. You care for animals, the environment, and just about every living creature. You also love serving other people and do things with a charitable cause.

Leo: As a highly receptive empath, you are significantly affected by the energies about you. For this reason, you constantly work hard to bring positivity to your environment which may get others to thinking you always long for the spotlight.

Virgo: You have a deep sense of connection with other people, making it easy working with you. You are born with a 'oneness' which others spend their lives trying to find. You can grow from even the slightest change.

Libra: There is a reason you love and care for animals, often more than you do for people. You are a fauna empath whose heart always feels for our friends from the animal world. You may have taken in strays and donated to shelters much more often than others.

Sagittarius: You have the ability to sense things from different astral planes. This makes you a wanderer. With this gift, you lend your help to whomever you deem needs it.

Scorpio: You're a chameleon empath who feels everything and is able to learn from things other people go through. But even though you take on much of their experiences, you are able to let those go and deal with your own emotions.

Capricorn: As a flora empath, you have special fondness of plants and nature. You tend to choose herbal medicines over conventional ones. This also makes you a sort of healer.

Aquarius: You're the kind of empath who always questions and seeks the meaning in everything. You value honesty and surround yourself with people who care for and matter to you. It's a give and take: they take care of you as well as you take care of them

Pisces: You are innately emotional and receptive. You take people's physical and emotional sufferings and are able to comfort them without words. Your mere presence and simple stroke of compassion can be enough to lighten the load they're carrying.

So, do you think your sign matches your empath type?

Chapter 3
The Importance of Understanding Astrology

"Astrology is a language." – Dane Rudhyar

While the statement above is true, most of us do not understand the language in which astrology is written, that's why we are still lost when trying to decode what our horoscope is telling us. Understanding astrology is important as it can lead you on the road of self-awareness and self-discovery; it helps you make wiser choices for a better, more fulfilling future; and it can also be your means of communicating with the divine.

However, when speaking of astrology, most people only know about their zodiac sign, also referred to as the sun sign or star sign, but humans are more complex than that. Besides your sun sign, many other factors influence your life. You have your rising sign, your moon sign, the houses representing different areas of your life, and the ever-changing patterns of the stars and planets.

The first step towards a better understanding of astrology is the unlocking of your birth chart. From this, a new world will open for you, where you can see things more clearly and grasp their meaning more accurately. For this first step, knowing the following will be essential.

Your Sun Sign

Your sun sign indicates who you really are deep down. It defines your character and who you are as a person. This is the most easily determined part of your natal chart and can be learned by simply knowing your birthday.

Aries: March 21 – April 19

Taurus: April 20 – May 20

Gemini: May 21 – June 20

Cancer: June 21 – July 22

Leo: July 23 – August 22

Virgo: August 23 – September 22

Libra: September 23 – October 22

Scorpio: October 23 – November 21

Sagittarius: November 22 – December 21

Capricorn: December 22 – January 19

Aquarius: January 20 – February 18

Pisces: February 19 – March 20

Your Rising Sign or Ascendant

If your sun sign signifies your true character or the essence of your being, your rising sun indicates the traits or the aura that you give off to the world. This is how you choose to present yourself to people and how other people see you. In other words, your rising sun is the 'mask' you wear in society.

Your rising sign, also called the *ascendant*, is the sign that was 'rising' or 'ascending' on the eastern horizon at the moment of your birth. Besides your birthday, you need to know your birth place in order to accurately determine your rising sign. Many places on the internet can help you calculate and uncover your ascendant by providing this information.

If you were born at the time of sunrise (around 4am to 6am), your rising sign and sun sign will be the same because the same part of the zodiac is rising on the eastern horizon at that moment. This also means that your true Self and what you show to other people will be practically alike. However, if you were born at other times of the day, a different sign would be rising over the eastern horizon.

So, for instance, your sun sign is the fiery, risk-taking Aries, but the sign that was rising on the horizon when you were born was the patient, peace-loving Taurus, you are a brave, impulsive person deep inside but people will be fooled by the soft, delicate character you show off.

Your Moon Sign

Your moon sign characterizes your emotional motivations. It affects your general personality and can be a key to understanding yourself on a deeper level. It is what drives you to become the individual that you want to be and grasping it can open your door to self-awareness.

Your moon sign is determined by the position of the moon at the time of your birth. Most people don't get the opportunity to see this part of you and likewise you scarcely get the chance to see theirs but finding out one another's can be helpful in creating deeper, longer-lasting connections with each other.

The Four Elements and the Three Modalities

The signs are grouped into four based on the essential elements they correspond to. Fire and air signs are the masculine or active signs, while the earth and water signs are the feminine or passive signs.

Fire Signs: Aries, Leo, Sagittarius

The element of fire corresponds with creation, confidence, inspiration, vitality, willfulness, exploration, trailblazing, and taking control. Fire burns, as much as it can be creative, it also has the tendency to become destructive. It can bring bad temper, anger, and a possible need to control or dominate others. Fire signs are ambitious, enthusiastic, passionate, emotional, and enterprising. They possess a great deal of physical energy and vitality.

Air Signs: Gemini, Aquarius, Libra

The element of air corresponds with analysis, logic, intellectualism, objectivity, philosophy, and a desire to make an impacting social change. It also relates to government, politics, public relations, communication, rational skepticism, thought, and the external compass of the self. Air signs are intellectual and more likely to practice higher education and demonstrate refined taste.

Earth Signs: Capricorn, Virgo, Taurus

The element of earth corresponds with pragmatism, stability, financial security, and practicality. It is related to building, construction, property, real estate, design, fashion, and wealth management. Earth signs are loyal, goal-oriented, utilitarian, and methodical. They complete tasks and get things done.

Water Signs: Pisces, Cancer, Scorpio

The element of water corresponds with artistic talent, intuition, psychic abilities, emotions, sensitivity, empathy, and self-protection. It brings compassion, emotional balance, nurturing energy, and the desire of helping others. Water signs are intuitive, emotional, imaginative, and impressionable. They can also be moody and hypersensitive.

The 12 signs of the zodiac are also categorized according to the three modes or modalities which denote a person's core nature based on the season he/she was born.

Cardinal Signs: Aries, Cancer, Capricorn, Libra

Cardinal signs are active, willful, enterprising, independent, and restless in both mind and body. They are leaders who like taking charge, setting rules, and implementing order. They pursue change and dislike limitations or restrictions.

Fixed Signs: Aquarius, Leo, Taurus, Scorpio

Fixed signs are determined and stubborn, have intense personas, like following rules, and tend to avert change. They have slower energy but are persistent, highly productive, and persevering. They seek to build and maintain order.

Mutable Signs: Pisces, Gemini, Sagittarius, Virgo

Mutable signs are versatile, resourceful, impressionable, adaptable, but often indecisive. They are free-spirited and carefree. They are critical thinkers and like to seek out progress and embrace change.

What the Planets Represent

Each planet represents a different facet of the personality, as follows:

Sun: the sense of self, identity, self-expression, the emanation of being with self-respect, dignity, and warmth

Moon: moods, feelings, needs, the quality of emotional life

Mercury: thinking, cognitive, verbal, communication skills, speech

Venus: beauty, all things we find attractive, beautiful, and desirable

Mars: self-assertion, drives, instincts, will, vital energy that stimulates achievement and activity

Jupiter: capacity for aspiration and planning, growth, adventure, social participation, conceptual understanding, the desire for expansion

Saturn: the desire for tangible achievements and security, social adaptation, traditionalism

Uranus: defiance, rebellion, unconventionality, expressing of one's uniqueness, radical or progressive politics, scientific pursuits, sudden change of attitude

Neptune: transcendence, spirituality, religion, development of psychic abilities, the desire for expansion of one's consciousness, a tendency towards avoidance, escapism, victim mentality, and helplessness

Pluto: catharsis, detoxification, letting go, removal of psychic impurities like greed, hatred, jealousy, and resentment

The Sun, the Moon, and the planets Mercury, Venus, and Mars are referred to as the "personal planets." Planets Jupiter and Saturn are the "social planets," and Uranus, Neptune, and Pluto are the "transpersonal planets."

Chapter 4
The 12 Houses of the Zodiac

First discovered by the Babylonians, the 12 houses of the zodiac are recognized by most astrologers today. Beginning with the first house of the Self, the houses expand outward into the community and beyond. The first 6 houses are referred to as the "personal houses," and the last 6 houses as the "interpersonal houses."

The 12 houses, with each one being ruled by a specific sign, represent different areas of life and are associated with different sets of traits. Planets move through these houses like they do with zodiac signs, influencing each house with their energy.

1st House: Self, Appearance, and First Impressions

Natural Ruler: Aries

The first house of the zodiac is the foundation of the self or personality. It begins the zodiac and rules all 'firsts': first impressions, appearance, fresh starts, new initiatives and beginnings.

Planets in the first house will influence the way you present yourself and the way people view you. It can indicate your behavior and your perspective of the world.

The starting edge of the first house, which is referred to as the 'ascendant' or your 'rising sun' determines how you look, your general personality, your complexion, and the condition of your body.

2nd House: Finances, Values, and Possessions

Natural Ruler: Taurus

The second house represents all matters relating to the material world and the physical environment. This includes money matters, material possessions, qualities that you enjoy, and your senses of touch, sight, smell, sound, and taste.

Planets in your second house will influence your financial standing, as well as your self-esteem. You can be particularly sentimental about your possessions and emotional about your finances if the moon occupies this house.

3rd House: Community, Communication, and Thought

Natural Ruler: Gemini

The third house covers all means of communication—thinking, talking, and devices (pages, cell phones, etc.). It also represents adaptation, change, transition, hand-eye coordination, and connection with others. 'Community' includes siblings, neighbors, schools, libraries, community affairs, and short journeys.

Planets in your third house will affect your memory, rational thought, nervous energy, and the way you respond or adapt to a new environment. Look to this house to have a better understanding of how you share and process information.

4th House: Family, Foundations, and Instincts

Natural Ruler: Cancer

Sitting at the bottom part of the zodiac wheel, the fourth house governs the 'foundation' of everything, including your home, basic security, privacy, your parents (especially your mother), and your children. This house reflects the things that bring you comfort the way you act in your home.

Cancer affects the other planets in the fourth house, indicating domestic influence. This house is also associated with instincts and intuition, nurturing, unconditional love, childhood roots, and your desire to build a firm foundation of safety and security within your life.

5th House: Creativity, Pleasure, and Romance

Natural Ruler: Leo

The fifth house rules self-expression, creativity, romance, color, and everything that makes us feel good. It can also indicate your need for attention and drama. Leo's influence challenges us to pursue all the things that give us pleasure with fervent vigor.

This house is commonly associated with motivation, enthusiasm, personal pleasure, and our desire for greater joy. It also influences our love affairs, our inner child, amusement, and all sorts of drama in our life.

6th House: Health, Service, and Order

Natural Ruler: Virgo

As the domain of order, health and service, the sixth house governs organization, schedules, routines, diet, fitness, hygiene, healthy lifestyle, providing care, and being of assistance and service to others. This house reveals how well you deal with adjustment and change, challenging you to maintain your well-being and seek competence.

Planets in the sixth house urge you to tackle health concerns and perform tasks in a certain way. It is also the house of work, duties, personal projects, and the need to construct and adhere to a plan that produces tangible and orderly results.

7th House: Business, Contracts, and Partnerships

Natural Ruler: Libra

The seventh house is concerned with long-term, binding relationships, both personal and business. This includes marriage, contracts, business deals, and workplace collaborations.

Planets in the house challenge us to develop deep and intimate relationships with other people, influencing the way we relate to others and the things we value in our relationships. The seventh house is also associated with cooperation, equality, public dealings, and awareness of one's identity, agreements, and a desire for intimate interactions.

8th House: Transformation, Reincarnation, and Mystery

Natural Ruler: Scorpio

The eighth house governs all of our major experiences: birth, personal growth, sex, transformation, evolution, death, and regeneration.

It also rules merged energies, mysteries, bonding at a deep level, and other people's money and property (e.g. investments, inheritances, real estate).

Planets placed in this house indicate the different facets of ourselves working more cooperatively with one another in order to attain greater success. This house also affects our sense of purpose and judgment. It encompasses revelations and innovations, and those who possess this house are likely to become innovative.

9th House: Adventure, Exploration, and Philosophy

Natural Ruler: Sagittarius

The ninth house is the domain of the higher mind, spiritual visions, religion, expansion of knowledge, freedom, long-distance travel, adventure, philosophy, ethics, morals, inspiration, and optimism. This house allows us to expand our philosophical horizons and understanding of the world. It is where we seek the truth through our own experiences.

Planets in this house indicate our unyielding to conventional restrictions and our desire to grasp larger concepts, which we can use to overcome more significant issues in our life. This is where we covet 'higher answers' to give us peace of mind.

10th House: Career, Social Status, and Public Image

Natural Ruler: Capricorn

The tenth house touches upon your ambitions, your relationship with tradition, and your place in the society. It rules corporations, structures, public image, honors, fame, awards, achievements, boundaries, discipline, authority, rules, and the paternal figures in one's life.

This house represents our capacity and motivation to make great contributions to the world, which would earn us recognition and respect. Planets in this house indicate a new professional role or reputation which will lead us to the fulfillment of our desires and needs.

11th House: Friendship, Groups, and Goals

Natural Ruler: Aquarius

The eleventh house indicates how we relate to the rest of the humankind. It encourages us to build strong relationships with the community and influences our interest in clubs, organizations, and groups.

Planets in this house are concerned with how we connect with groups or friends and with the need to have our actions valued or accepted. This house is also associated with ambitions, aspirations, shared ideals, originality, eccentricity, surprises, inventions, all things futuristic, and the impulse to make the world a better place.

12th House: Inner Growth, Self-Undoing, and Conclusions

Natural Ruler: Pisces

The twelfth and final house rules endings, healing, introspection, and your inner depths. It represents how we deal with and explore our deepest thoughts in silence and solitude. This is where we build our inner strength to conquer our fears, sorrows, and limitations.

Planets on this house have a subtle influence because the house works on a subconscious level of the mind. This house is also associated with spirituality, psychic sensitivity, the need for alone time, hidden awareness and understandings, omens, the subconscious, the afterlife, completions, old age, surrender, and tying up loose ends.

Chapter 5
Equinoxes, Solstices, and the Zodiac

We've probably all heard about equinoxes and solstices, but many of us do not know exactly what they are, how they come about, how they relate to astrology, and how they implicate our lives. This chapter will dig into this subject so that you can better understand how these astronomical events can influence your life and even our planet.

The first thing you need to remember about equinoxes and solstices is that they signify the beginning of each season. The two equinox points mark the start of autumn and spring, while the two solstice points mark the start of winter and summer. Each of the points corresponds to the one of the four cardinal signs—also called the cardinal axis, where you can find the strong angles in your birth chart.

Those angles are highly sensitive points that trigger major events in your life.

The different seasons are caused by the earth's tilting on its axis. Throughout an entire year, either the northern or southern hemisphere becomes more exposed to the sun. And at two separate occasions, the sun reaches its lowest or highest point in the sky at noontime. These events give us spring equinox, summer solstice, autumnal equinox, and winter solstice.

The Spring (Vernal) & Fall (Autumnal) Equinoxes

Equinox is the time or date at which the sun passes the celestial equator (the invisible circle that is on the same place as the Earth's equator). This happens twice per year, with spring equinox signifying the start of spring and autumnal equinox signifying the end of summer. During this time, the center of the sun goes above and below the horizon at an equal duration of the day, regardless of your location on Earth. This results in the length of nighttime and daytime being equal, hence the term *equinox* (which translates to "equal night").

The spring or vernal equinox starts on March 21, marking the beginning of a new astrological year as the sun enters Aries. This period is often associated with new beginnings and fresh starts. The fall or autumnal equinox begins on September 21 when the sun enters the sign Libra. This is typically a time to "harvest" and reap the fruits of one's labor. It also introduces an impression to conserve resources and energy as nights become longer than they are during other times of the year.

The Summer & Winter Solstices

Like an equinox, a solstice occurs twice per year—at the start of winter and at the beginning of summer. At either of these two points, the sun reaches its lowest or maximum elevation relative to the celestial equator, giving us the shortest and the longest days of the year. *Solstice* literally translates to "Sun stands still."

The summer solstice begins on June 21 and correlates to the sign Cancer. During this period, the sun appears to stop and then begins to slowly decline southward. Summer solstice gives us longer hours of daylight because at this period, the sun stops over the northernmost point (the Tropic of Cancer), illuminating the northern hemisphere more than the southern hemisphere.

The winter solstice, occurring on December 21, correlates to the sign Capricorn. This period is when the sun looks to be stopping at the southernmost point (the Tropic of Capricorn) and begins to move slowly towards north. As the North Pole is tilted away from the sun during this time, the northern hemisphere receives less light than the southern hemisphere, giving us the shortest days of the year. The winter solstice is associated with rebirth and renewed hope.

Cardinal Signs Begin the Seasons

It is no accident that solstices and equinoxes all correlate to the cardinal signs of the zodiac. Cardinal signs signal the beginning of each season; thus they are associated with prospects of initiative and regeneration. When the Sun enters a cardinal sign, we are to celebrate the beginning of something new—be it a solstice or an equinox—and each season corresponds to a specific and vital function that we can rely on. The solstice and equinox points are perhaps the Divine's clue for us, leaving dots which we only need to connect to unfold the mystery behind our planet's never-ending cycle of life.

Chapter 6
When the Planets Rotate

Planets move slowly along the zodiac every day. As they do, they pass through the 12 houses of the natal horoscope, influencing the house for the duration of its stay. The daily changes in our life are influenced by the transits of the inner, faster-moving planets (Sun to Mars) as their transits are measured in days or weeks. Whereas, the transits of the outer, slower-moving planets (Jupiter to Pluto) measured in years or decades, bring about long-term effects in our lives. Transiting planets in retrograde also influence the duration of the transit effect. Planets can stay in retrograde motion from 21 days to 5 months.

Transit of the Sun: The influence of the transiting sun stimulates the activities of the house it occupies, and either weakens or intensifies the planetary effects depending on the aspect of the Sun to the natal planet.

Transit of the Moon: As the moon spends only two to three days in a house, its effects are too quick (usually a matter of few hours only) that you rather feel them as unconscious impulses than conscious responses to a situation. You may or may not be consciously aware of its transit effects, but you certainly will feel them.

Transit of Planet Mercury: During Mercury's stay in a house (which lasts about a week), you will feel its influence on your mental outlook, urges to travel, and communication with others. When transiting, Mercury is in retrograde; it may cause delays in the activities that it affects.

Transit of Planet Venus: As the planet of material pleasures and love, Venus's transit brings about enjoyment of various sorts. You will feel its effects more as subjective feelings rather than fuels for action.

Transit of Planet Mars: Spending about two months in a natal house, Mars gives off energies that fuel you to chase after your desires and needs. If Mars is in retrograde when transiting, which can last for three months, you may encounter delays or reversals in the activities that Mars influences.

Transit of Planet Jupiter: Jupiter spends about a year in each house, affecting your expansive feelings and providing opportunities to broaden your horizons. Jupiter goes in retrograde motion for about four months.

Transit of Planet Uranus: Uranus spends about seven years in each house and becomes retrograde for five months. Its transit causes considerable changes in terms of breaking up your past and putting the pieces back together in a more practical way, allowing you to live your present more meaningfully.

Transit of Planet Neptune: Neptune spends about five months in each house. During such time, it opens you up to new discoveries where you can use your creativity in the areas influenced by the house that Neptune occupies. Its effects may also empower your psychic abilities, which consequently may weaken your ability to differentiate reality and illusion in the same affected areas.

Transit of Planet Pluto: Being the slowest-moving planet, Pluto stays in each house for about twenty years and becomes retrograde for about five months. Its effects bring new beginnings and major transformations in the affairs influenced by the house occupied by Pluto.

Planets in Retrograde

If there is an 'R' beside a planet in your natal chart, it means that that planet was in retrograde at the time of your birth. A planet is retrograde when it appears to be going backward in its motion instead of moving direct. 'Appears' because it is physically impossible for a planet to travel backward in its orbit. It only gives the illusion of moving backwards because the Earth is moving faster passed it.

Here is an analogy: Have someone walk at a normal pace ahead of you. Then, start running. Observe how the person moves relative to you. As you run towards him, he appears to be moving away and he is, but as you run passed him, he appears to be moving backward from your point of view when actually he is still walking forward at the same pace.

While their movement is a mere illusion, retrograde planets have real effects to which astrologers and believers in astrology can attest to. The areas ruled by the planet in retrograde can become weak, troublesome, or challenging during the cycle. But instead of looking at retrograde with such a negative light, why don't we take them as an opportunity to dig up old ideas you have set aside, revisit old experiences, resolve unsettled arguments, and reconnect with old friends. Retrograde shift our attention back to the past, giving us the chance to finish the things we started and strengthening our plans to make sure we move forward on a firm foundation.

Below, you will find how the different retrograde can affect our lives daily or in the long-term. It also gives helpful suggestions on what to do best to make the most of each retrograde. Note that all the other eight planets in the solar system retrograde; the sun and the moon never become retrograde.

Mercury Retrograde: Mercury—the planet of transportation, communication, technology and travel—is the most commonly known retrograde. The planet goes in such motion three to four times per year, lasting about 21 days each cycle. During such time, communication seems to slow down, technology goes haywire, misunderstandings and arguments arise, cars suddenly break down, computers crash, and things don't seem to go as planned.

As Mercury also concerns the mind, the speech and thinking patterns, people who were born with Mercury in retrograde generally have an introverted or reflective mind. They think things over several times before coming to a conclusion and they take in information quite differently than others.

What to do during this retrograde?

Catch up with old friends and acquaintances. Back up all digital files and devices. Postpone business deals. Resume an old course or writing project. Clear up your thoughts, and plan to explain or repeat yourself a few times more than usual.

Venus Retrograde: Venus goes retrograde for 4 to 6 weeks every 18 months, during which weak links in romantic relationships are revealed and past illicit affairs are brought back. When the love planet is retrograde, astrologers caution about weddings, proposals, and other major moves concerning love relationships.

People with Venus retrograde in their birth chart are deep-feeling in nature and take socializing often seriously. They consider love as extremely important but may not always be explicit as to show to others how deeply they love. They may also be prone to self-sabotage in that they may have an underlying impression that they don't need love or aren't lovable enough.

What to do in this retrograde?

Mend any issues that hinder your way to love or jeopardize your relationship. Identify if you have the right match; if not, let it go and move on. Gain closure with a past lover or reunite if the pieces fit. Make amends with a woman in your life.

Mars Retrograde: Mars—the planet that rules wars—goes retrograde for about two months every two years and in such time conflicts and fighting can come about. One's normal vitality and energy are depleted, therefore initiating an activity or undertaking a new enterprise may not be the best idea during this period.

People born under this retrograde have the tendency to develop a fear of being ineffective as they see it as a challenge to assert or stand up for themselves. Competition can be unnerving, and they would often choose to set their own pace rather than working under other people's terms.

What to do in this retrograde?

Practice patience. Learn to deal with stress and pressure more effectively. Resolve conflicts through compromise. Let go of resentments and lay your weapon down. Slow down to avoid accidents. Review your goals. Get back to your old sport or workout routine. Make amends with a man in your life.

Jupiter Retrograde: Jupiter is retrograde for about 4 months per year. While most of the other retrograde seem to have alarming effects, Jupiter retrograde is rather forgiving. It allows more room for error and welcomes experimentation (though make sure you learn from those slip-ups). It may inspire impatience but perhaps it is simply telling us to move towards our goals in slow motion, especially when we aren't exactly sure how to reach those goals.

People with Jupiter retrograde in their birth chart generally have unusual belief systems, set of morals, and perspectives in life. They choose to learn from their own mishaps and experiences. As they don't believe in luck, they lay out plans but then worry about the consequences of their own actions.

What to do in this retrograde?

Slow down and evaluate your actions first before rushing into things. Travel to old favorite places. Take on an abandoned business venture. Finish a deferred certification or degree in school.

Saturn Retrograde: Saturn is the taskmaster planet that rules delay, caution, limitation, responsibility, authority, discipline, rules, regulations, control, denial, pain, and fear. It goes retrograde for about 4 and a half months per year. During this period, astrologers advise against starting new projects, yielding to authority, over scheduling, and taking unnecessary risks. Use this time to reassess your relationships and commitments.

Being born during a Saturn retrograde can mean having experiences of self-doubt and guilt every so often. They tend to keep their fears within themselves and cover up their vulnerability by putting on a brave face. They may also have a fear of not effectively carrying out their responsibilities and letting people down.

What to do in this retrograde?

Practice respect and self-discipline. Spend your money wisely. Reconsider your career path and goals. Hold back instant gratification. Work through paternal issues and appreciate all the relationships you have.

Uranus Retrograde: When Uranus is retrograde, which occurs for about 5 to 6 months each year, things aren't guaranteed, and loose ends may surface out of the blue. People's perspectives and thinking patterns also change dramatically during this period. On the other hand, Uranus retrograde may lead us to a new level of being.

Uranus retrograde can indicate fears of change or distrust of new improvements or technology breakthroughs. People born with this retrograde tend to hide their unconventionalities, whereas those who are born Uranus direct are more inclined to show them off.

What to do in this retrograde?

Study up on current events, scientific breakthroughs, and politics. Do activities with humanitarian cause. Rethink your stance in politics. Make sure you're standing up for something good and not just being defiant for no reason. Cut yourself out from people who bring more trouble to your life.

Neptune Retrograde: Neptune, the planet of dreams, personal possibilities, and spirituality, goes retrograde for about 5 months per year. When Neptune is direct, it gives us a big picture of life's truth and allows us to tap into our dreams and intuition. But when it is in retrograde, ignoring the truth becomes more difficult. Neptune retrograde can be a harsh wake-up call but this can lead us to discovering the things that really matter to us.

Those born with Neptune retrograde hide their compassion, vulnerabilities, and spiritual side as they do not feel comfortable expressing them and they can be naturally distrustful. These people may not be inclined to dreaming big dreams because of their fear of disappointments.

What to do in this retrograde?

Pick up an old artistic or musical project. Delve into your subconscious. Question your beliefs and explore your spirituality. Do therapy and healing activities. Get rid of toxic people in your life. Meditate.

Pluto Retrograde: Pluto is retrograde for 5 months, and this can be a time for personal reckoning but a time for purging a lot of things, too. As Pluto rules transformations, we can work on improving ourselves and changing our negative traits. Pluto retrograde may shed light on the dark corners of your experiences, which you might need to revisit and confront in order to grow.

Those with Pluto retrograde in their chart may have a fear of being betrayed, controlled, or manipulated by others, but they tend to keep these to themselves as telling others their fears makes them feel even more vulnerable. They have this need to be in control which they aren't vocal about.

What to do in this retrograde?

Revisit old fears and delve into your personal "shadow side" with a more open mind. Eliminate toxic energies, clear your space, and clean the clutter.

Distance yourself from situations and people that might put you at risk. Resolve the issues of being bullied or dominated and watch out that you may not overpower other people. Explore the mystical parts of your being via past-life regression; you may work with a medium in doing so.

Each retrograde has a "shadow period"—that tricky period where the planet goes from forward motion to the apparent backward motion, and vice versa (sometimes these periods are referred to as the pre-retrograde and post-retrograde shadow). For this reason, you may feel the effects of a retrograde two weeks before it actually begins or after it has officially ended.

All planets become retrograde periodically. As it is inevitable, we must embrace it as an opportunity for building character. Sometimes, all it takes is a challenge for us to develop the self-awareness and the inner strength we need to grow and evolve as human beings.

Chapter 7
Survival Tips for the Hypersensitive

So now, we have learned how practically all the celestial bodies and phenomena can affect our lives on this planet. As empaths, having this knowledge helps us understand ourselves and why we feel the way we do. Understanding is part of the awareness of who we are and knowing who we really are is imperative in discovering our true purpose here on Earth.

Being an empath is tough enough and having the stars and planets go against your will can make it even tougher. We might not be able to dictate our stars, but we certainly can do a lot of things to mold and improve ourselves no matter what the heavenly circumstances bring about. Some days can be rough and may make you feel too dejected to stand up again, but know that everything around you and above you moves; the sun will rise again tomorrow, and it's going to be another hopeful day.

So, with that said, here are some survival tips for all of you, hypersensitive souls. Make sure to put all of these to use for you to maximize your abilities while still being able to live a happy and fulfilled life.

1. Watch out for energy vampires.

Have you ever been around certain people and felt drained without even talking or interacting with them? If so, then start identifying those people and distance yourself from them as much as possible. Your ability to become an emotional sponge can heighten around energy vampires, overwhelming you with negative energies and preventing you from absorbing positive emotions. Surround yourself with love and peace and let your body assimilate them.

2. Create an energy shield.

There are situations in which you would rather avoid a person you know is draining you, but you just can't because of their important role in your life. Family gatherings, social events, and important work functions can involve people and undesirable energies you find hard to handle.

In such circumstances, you will need to activate your "energy shield" to deflect toxic energies away. It can take a lot of practice to learn to create a mental barrier but once you've established this, you will be able to let in only those you want to let in and keep unwanted visitors at bay.

To create an energy shield, visualize a bubble or a white light enveloping your entire being. Nothing passes this shield unless you allow it. When you feel like the occasion or the people are starting to drain you, retreat into this shield and regain your balance.

3. Be careful how you use your energy.

As an empath's energy can be easily drained, it is important that you prioritize how you use your limited supply. It is in your nature to be always on the run to help others but doing this too much can deplete your energy fast. Reserve your supplies for those who will truly appreciate your effort and who genuinely wish to improve their lives.

You can't be everyone's hero and make everyone else happy at all times. Do not waste your time and effort trying to help people who would rather wallow in their misery and drain your energy for naught. Sometimes, the best thing you can do is to let them help themselves.

4. Watch over your thoughts.

If you have not established your energy shield to ward off external negativity, the next best thing you can do is to watch over the thoughts that fill your mind and identify whether it's really yours or someone else's. For instance, when you suddenly find yourself deep in depressing thoughts, ask yourself whether it's your sadness or just something you've soaked up from another.

The key here is *identification*. Keep close watch of your thoughts or feelings and identify the source. Once you've worked that out, then you will be able to find a solution to dispel that energy before it gets the best of you.

5. Make time for downtime.

As it can be hard for empaths to refuse helping others and they can be exhausted easily by others' emotional needs. They need a lot of down-time to recharge their batteries. Do activities that you find restorative—it can be reading, meditating, knitting, or cooking. You may also hit the trail and do mountain biking or take long walks. Listen to your body to find the activities that best suit you. Do not feel bad about saying no to people sometimes. Your well-being should be a high priority.

6. Forgive and be grateful.

As a highly sensitive person, you may have found yourself feeling hurt and used more than others and may sometimes feel cursed for having empathic abilities. But holding on to past hurts and not wholeheartedly accepting yourself can drain your life source. Learn to release your grudges, let go of your hurtful past, and forgive whomever has wronged you. Be thankful for your gifts; though it can be burdening sometimes, it has precious benefits which others can only wish to have. With genuine forgiveness and gratefulness, you can relieve yourself of all the negative energies that have accrued inside you and begin your healing process.

7. Set healthy boundaries.

If staying away from energy vampires or creating an energy shield is not always possible, learn to set boundaries whenever necessary. Limit how much time you spend talking or listening to stressful people and nicely cut them off if they get mean or critical. Boundaries can be temporal, conversational, or physical, depending on how they invade your energy.

8. Create a safe and welcoming place.

Recover your energy and regain your balance quicker by creating a comfortable, welcoming place in which you can relax. It can be your bedroom, bathroom, garden, or anywhere quiet and inviting. Do not take calls, watch TV, or ponder over the issues in your life. Designate it as a place for healing and relaxation only.

9. Spend time in nature.

Empaths have a natural connection with the Earth and being exposed to nature can be a powerful healing method for them. Nature is brimming with vitality and vibrant energy and by simply immersing in it even for a while, you will be able to absorb this energy and regenerate yourself.

10. Bury the negativity.

Still using your strong connection with nature to your advantage, you can send your downbeat feelings and energy into the Earth and let it absorb them and, similarly, it can also send some positive vibrations upwards into your core. This may take some practice to effectively carry out, but the results can be really helpful to an empath. Learn to identify and strengthen your bond with the Earth and it can either furnish you with replenished energy or take your burden and bury them for you.

11. Use positive affirmations.

People with empathic abilities are generally giving, open, and kind-hearted, but this does not necessarily mean they remain positive at all times. Because they can take on the energies around them, sometimes without them realizing it, they can struggle with anger, grief, sadness, and other destructive emotions that aren't even theirs. To maintain positivity, carrying a bag of positive affirmations can be helpful. Repeat a chosen affirmation (one that best suits your current situation) and feel the negative vibes swim away and a positive light shine upon you.

12. Meditate.

The power of meditation is undisputable. For empaths, it can be a great way to heal, find balance, and take stock of emotions. Starting this practice can be hard because it seems like you are letting yourself be alone wallowing in your thoughts. However, practicing meditation can allow you to become more aware of what is going on in your mind and body, and help you sort your own emotions from those of others. Commit to meditating regularly, starting with a few minutes per day if you are new to it. It will bring about vast benefits to your life in different aspects.

People and situations can drain you but the nature, the love and peace that can be anywhere, the comfort of the people you care about, and the awareness that lies inside you, can shower you with replenished energy, letting you move on with life with renewed vitality and revived motivation.

Conclusion

I'd like to thank you for taking the time to read through my words!

I hope this book was able to help you expand your understanding and awareness of yourself and of everything and everyone around you. Empathy and astrology are interesting subjects that make us see more clearly the deeper we delve into ourselves and make more sense of our existence on this planet, the further we travel through the heavens.

The next step is to start looking within yourself, and learn to accept everything that comes with that, both the good and the not-so-good. These are qualities which make us who we are and any weaknesses we have can also become strengths.

It is common that empaths can sometimes feel like something is wrong with them and how it is such a burden being themselves. If you think that, then start telling yourself that you are exactly who you are supposed to be and that there is absolutely nothing wrong with you. You are not like most people because you are an extraordinary human being who is meant for something bigger and something more significant.

Discover yourself through your stars and you will know what I mean. So, you can go ahead meet with an astrologer and get started with your birth chart today!

I wish you the best of luck!

77312410R00042

Made in the USA
Middletown, DE
19 June 2018